FAIRACRES PUBLICATIONS 231

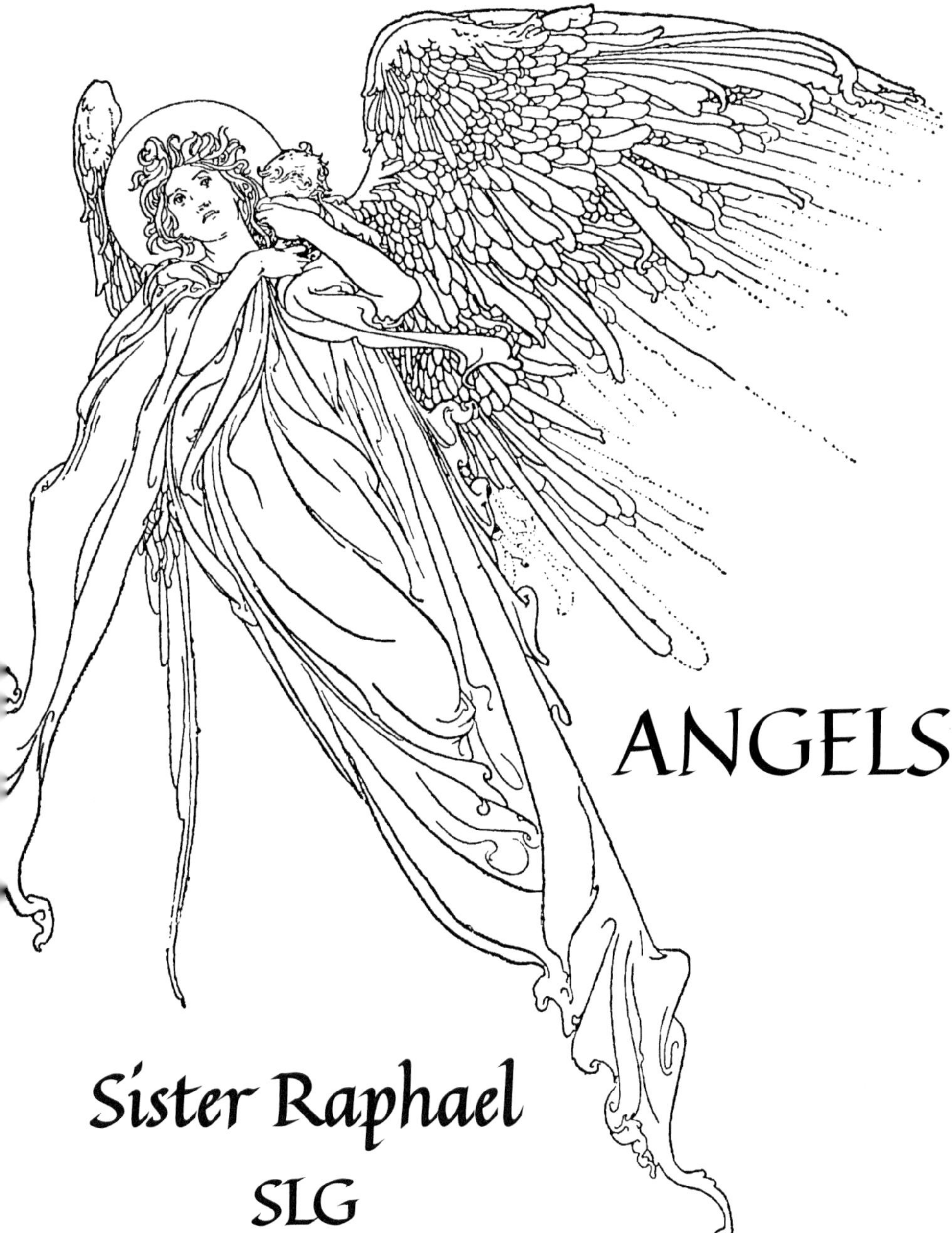

ANGELS

Sister Raphael
SLG

SLG Press

© 2025 SLG Press
First Edition 2025

Fairacres Publications No. 231

Print ISBN 978-0-7283-0422-2
Fairacres Publications Series ISSN 0307-1405

SLG Press asserts the right of Sister Raphael SLG to be identified as the author of this work in accordance with the Copyright, Designs and Patents Act 1988.

All rights reserved. No part of this publication may be reproduced, stored in a retrieval system, or transmitted, in any form or by any means, electronic, mechanical, photocopying, recording or otherwise, without the prior permission of the copyright owner.

Edited, designed and typeset in Palatino Linotype by Julia Craig-McFeely

Biblical quotations are taken from the New Revised Standard Version of the Bible unless otherwise noted in the text.

Cover Image: Franz Xaver Zettler (1841–1916), 'Angel Windows', stained glass, 1908, Chapel of Our Lady of Zion, Cathedral of the Madeleine, Salt Lake City, Utah (photo: Nate Bergin CC-BY-4.0), edited detail.

SLG Press
Convent of the Incarnation
Fairacres • Oxford
www.slgpress.co.uk

Printed by
BCQ Solutions Ltd, Buckingham

CONTENTS

Introduction 1
Archangels 9
Archangel Michael 12
Archangel Gabriel 15
Archangel Raphael 18
Archangel Uriel 21
Holy Guardian Angels 23
Lucifer and his Angels 26
The Heavenly Host 29
Angels in the Scriptures 32
Angel Prayers and Quotations 39
Picture Credits 44

ANGELS

INTRODUCTION

Angel voices ever singing
round Thy throne of light,
angel harps, forever ringing,
rest not day nor night;
thousands only live to bless Thee
and confess thee Lord of might.

Francis Pott (1832–1909)
'Angel-Voices Ever Singing', NEH 336, v. 1

Have you ever thought about how many times in general conversation the word 'angel' is used?

'Be an angel and feed the dog.'

'My friend was an absolute angel to me when I was ill. I could not have managed without her.'

'Look at him—so angelic, little cherub.'

I expect we have all heard, or made, similar remarks without any thought of angels themselves, and certainly not as holy, heavenly beings who constantly worship around the throne of God. In these angel expressions we use so freely there is always an element of generosity, kindness and love. We love the little

cherub. We are appreciative and thankful for the generosity of the friend who cared for us when we were unwell and thank God for them. If we are asked to perform a kindness, let us do it cheerfully, to the glory of God.

In this book I remind us of the presence of angels throughout Scripture, not just as passing expressions of appreciation for someone's kindness. Angels are so often there that we are inclined to forget them, or see them as 'part of the furniture'; yet in many cultures, Christian and other, they serve a greater purpose and remind us of aspects of our lives and our relationship with God that we are apt to forget. So this book is about angels, to remind us to think of them and all that they mean.

We are told that, even at the end of time, there will be angels present, so we should never discount or ignore them.

> Then the sign of the Son of Man will appear in heaven, and then all the tribes of the earth will mourn, and they will see 'the Son of Man coming on the clouds of heaven' with power and great glory. And he will send out his angels with a loud trumpet call, and they will gather his elect from the four winds, from one end of heaven to the other. (Matt. 24:30–1)

We may never see an angel, but we know from Scripture they are ever present. Jacob dreamed of angels coming and going between heaven and the earth:

> … he dreamed that there was a ladder set up on the earth, the top of it reaching to heaven; and the angels of God were ascending and descending on it. (Gen. 28:12)

Then Jacob heard a voice speaking to him, which he realized was God, telling him about the next part of his journey of life. Jacob said:

> How awesome is this place! This is none other than the house of God, and this is the gate of heaven. (Gen. 28:17)

We may have had similar experiences and have known instinctively that we were in a holy place.

What do angels look like?

Saint Augustine in the fourth century said angels were made of light, while Thomas Aquinas in the thirteenth thought of them as compressed air. We may think of angels in human form, particularly when they are described in the Bible. The most familiar are probably the description of the angel—or angels—waiting at the empty tomb of Christ after the Resurrection:

> And suddenly there was a great earthquake; for an angel of the Lord, descending from heaven, came and rolled back the stone and sat on it. His appearance was like lightning, and his clothing white as snow. (Matt. 28:2–3)

> As they entered the tomb, they saw a young man, dressed in a white robe, sitting on the right side … (Mark 16:5)

> … suddenly two men in dazzling clothes stood beside them. The women were terrified and bowed their faces to the ground, but the men said to them, 'Why do you look for the living among the dead? He is not here, but has risen.' (Luke 24:4–5)

> … and she [Mary Magdalen] saw two angels in white, sitting where the body of Jesus had been lying, one at the head and the other at the feet. (John 20:12)

And then at the Ascension:

> While he was going and they were gazing up toward heaven, suddenly two men in white robes stood by them. They said, 'Men of Galilee, why do you stand looking up toward heaven? This Jesus, who has been taken up from you into heaven, will come in the same way as you saw him go into heaven.' (Acts 1:10–11)

These are the most consistent and vivid descriptions of angels in the Gospels: always men wearing bright white clothes.

These descriptions suggest that angels have a particular real-world appearance, but it is more likely that this was a human attempt to make sense of something outside of their experience. White clothing in biblical times, as now, was a sign of purity and holiness. Today a Christening robe is pure white, and white is also worn for other important occasions.

> Yet you have still a few persons in Sardis who have not soiled their clothes; they will walk with me, dressed in white, for they are worthy. If you conquer, you will be clothed like them in white robes … (Rev. 3:4–5)

The Essenes, a very strict Jewish ascetic community around the time of Jesus, embraced a number of practices of spiritual and material purity that included wearing only white garments, so it is not surprising that angels should be visualized dressed in white. Father Gilbert Shaw explains our wish to create an appearance for angels that we can relate to our own experience:

I know of an occasion in dealing with a place under an infestation of evil forces, when the minister concerned invoked an angel at the beginning of the prayers. The intercessor with him suddenly exclaimed 'Do you see the angel?' It happened that the minister himself was conscious of the arrival of a presence of spirit. The intercessor was recalled then and there to the business in hand which was prayer and not seeing angels; yet afterwards from the evidential point of view it seemed interesting to inquire what had been seen. The description offered was analogous to a Burne-Jones figure, obviously because the intercessor was an artist and had clothed the sense of presence from the memory of pictures which had impressed the idea of 'angel' on the mind.*

The depiction of Angels having wings appears early in the Bible: angels, cherubim and seraphim—winged creatures—are described in Isaiah 6. In his vision of 'God in the Temple' Isaiah saw the Lord on his throne:

> Seraphs were in attendance above him; each had six wings: with two they covered their faces, and with two they covered their feet, and with two they flew.   (Is. 6:2)

That may be how we picture angels, but they are not persons in the way that we are humans, even though it seems that, like us, they eat food. In Psalm 78, verse 25, we find the line 'Mortals ate of the bread of angels; he sent them food in abundance.'

---

* Gilbert Shaw, 'Angels and Demons in Human Life', in *The Angels of Light and the Powers of Darkness: A Symposium,* ed. Eric Mascall (Fellowship of St Alban and St Sergius, 1954), 53–4.

What are angels? They are spirits who work for God, bringing his messages to us, and taking our responses to God, whether they are of happiness, sorrow, joy, tears, good works, or thanksgiving.

> I do not think you can prove from first principles the existence of angels. ... What I do think is that a worldview that excludes as impossible or ridiculous the presence of unseen spiritual companions is a worldview that will also exclude much of what is valuable in human life. If we are to take human beings seriously and as belonging in this world, we must have a sense of a world in which there are spiritual realities. There can be goodness and truth. There can be both meaning and mystery. A worldview which has room for the human spirit will always leave the door ajar for the angels to slip in. Conversely, if we maintain a worldview that leaves room for the angels then we will have one that also leaves room for the fullest meaning of human life.*

May we join with the angels in praise and worship by day and by night, now and always, just as we are invited to join with the angels and saints during the Eucharist, before we say or sing the Sanctus.

---

* David Albert Jones, 'Angels as a Guide to Ethics', *The Pastoral Review*, 4/1 (2007), 11–16.

ARCHANGELS

Christ, the fair glory of the holy angels,
Thou who hast made us, who o'er us rulest,
Grant of thy mercy, unto us thy servants
Steps up to heaven.

Rabanus Maurus (*c*. 776-856), trans. Percy Dearmer (1867–1936)
hymn for St Michael and All Angels, NEH 190, v. 1

We are told that some angels are more important than others, or lead other angels. There are only two biblical passages that use the word 'archangel', both in the New Testament, in Jude and in 1 Thessalonians:

> For the Lord himself, with a cry of command, with the archangel's call and with the sound of God's trumpet, will descend from heaven, and the dead in Christ will rise first.
> (1 Thess. 4:16)

> But when the archangel Michael contended with the devil and disputed about the body of Moses, he did not dare to bring a condemnation of slander against him, but said, 'The Lord rebuke you!' (Jude 9)

In the Old Testament, the angels who are usually referred to as archangels in English, are given the title of *śārīm* ('princes'), to show their superior rank and status. In Daniel 8:11, Gabriel is described as a 'prince of the host' of angels. Daniel continues:

> So Michael, one of the chief princes, came to help me, and I left him there … There is no one with me who contends against these princes except Michael, your prince. … At that time Michael, the great prince, the protector of your people, shall arise. (Dan. 10:13, 21; 12:1)

Archangels appear in many traditions drawn from Scripture, hymns and spiritual books. Their names all end in '-el', meaning in Hebrew 'of God' or 'from God'. They come from Hebrew scriptures, apocryphal texts or even folklore and include Sariel (Command of God), Raguel (Friend of God), Remiel (Mercy of God), Sealtiel (Intercessor of God), Jegudiel (Glorifier of God), Barachiel (Blessed by God, often depicted holding a white rose in his hand against his breast) and Jerahmiel (God's exaltation, venerated as an inspirer and awakener of exalted thoughts that raise a person toward God (2 Esdras 4:36)). Before he was cast out, Satan was called Sataniel. In post-medieval Jewish mysticism there are traditionally twelve archangels, who are each assigned to a certain *sephira* (sphere): Shubael, Raziel, Cassiel, Zadkiel, Camael, Michael, Uriel, Haniel, Raphael, Jophiel, Gabriel, and Azrael. The *Life of Adam and Eve*[*] lists the archangels Michael, Gabriel, Uriel, Raphael and Joel.

---

[*] A Jewish apocryphal group of writings also known in its Greek version as *The Apocalypse of Moses*. It recounts the lives of Adam and Eve from their expulsion from the Garden of Eden to their deaths. It provides more detail about the Fall of Man, including Eve's version of the story.

In most Christian denominations we recognize four archangels. Only the first three are named in the canonical Christian Bible, but the fourth is usually considered to be Uriel:

MICHAEL (in Hebrew 'Who is like God?' or 'Gift from God') has been depicted from earliest Christian times as a warrior or defender, who holds in his right hand a spear with which he attacks Lucifer, and in his left hand a green palm branch. Michael is especially considered to be the Guardian of the Orthodox Faith and a fighter against heresies.

GABRIEL (in Hebrew 'God is my strength' or 'Might of God') is the messenger and herald of the mysteries of God, especially the Incarnation, and a guiding strength. He is usually depicted holding a lantern with a lighted taper inside it in his right hand, and in his left hand a mirror of green jasper signifying the wisdom of God as a hidden mystery.

RAPHAEL (in Hebrew 'God heals') is the healer and curer of ills. Raphael is only named in the book of Tobit and is usually depicted leading Tobias as a child with one hand and with a physician's alabaster jar in the other.

URIEL (in Hebrew 'Light of God') appears in 2 Esdras 4:1 and 5:20. He is the bringer of light, and is usually depicted holding a sword in his right hand, and a flame in his left.

These angels are described in more detail in the following pages.

ARCHANGEL MICHAEL

The feast of St Michael and all the Angels is on 29 September.

Michael appears several times in the Book of Daniel, and twice in the New Testament, in Jude verse 9 (quoted on page 10) and in Revelation chapter 12. In the book of Revelation there are many appearances of angels, notably the seven who serve around the throne of God:

> When the Lamb opened the seventh seal, there was silence in heaven for about half an hour. And I saw the seven angels who stand before God, and seven trumpets were given to them.
>
> Another angel with a golden censer came and stood at the altar; he was given a great quantity of incense to offer with the prayers of all the saints on the golden altar that is before the throne. And the smoke of the incense, with the prayers of the

> saints, rose before God from the hand of the angel. Then the angel took the censer and filled it with fire from the altar and threw it on the earth; and there were peals of thunder, rumblings, flashes of lightning, and an earthquake.
>
> (Rev. 8:1–5)

To put events into context it helps to read Revelation, chapters 1–12. In chapter 12:7–17 the well-known story of St Michael and the dragon (the devil) is written, the subject of many illustrations over the centuries:

> And war broke out in heaven; Michael and his angels fought against the dragon. The dragon and his angels fought back, but they were defeated, and there was no longer any place for them in heaven. The great dragon was thrown down, that ancient serpent, who is called the Devil and Satan, the deceiver of the whole world—he was thrown down to the earth, and his angels were thrown down with him. (Rev. 12:7–9)

When we are troubled by the many cares and problems that come upon us in this earthly life, perhaps it would help to think of them as our particular 'dragons'.

Relating this to our own lives, what might an angel be saying to the Church today—to communities, to families, to us? Perhaps, as a prayer, we may use a verse of the hymn 'Christ, the Fair Glory of the Holy Angels', the hymn for Michaelmas:

> Send thy archangel, Michael, to our succour;
> Peacemaker blessed, may he banish from us
> Striving and hatred, so that for the peaceful
> All things may prosper.
>
> Athelstan Riley (1858–1945)
> 'Christ, the Fair Glory of the Holy Angels', NEH 190, v. 2

Reading, praying and meditating on mere words can bring us much encouragement as we let go and let God do for us all that he longs to do for us, and give to us, on our journey through life.

Saint Michael is the patron saint of many churches all over the world. There are many stories and incidents attributed to him other than biblical ones. Different traditions describe Michael as the angel who conquers in war, or who works miracles; he is almost always depicted as a warrior carrying a sword or spear, sometimes wearing armour.

Prayer

Eternal Lord God,
who ordained and constituted the
service of angels and men in a
wonderful order; grant that as your
holy angels always serve you in
heaven, so by your appointment
they may help and defend us
on earth; through Jesus Christ your
Son our Lord, who lives and reigns
with you and the Holy Spirit,
One God, now and for ever. Amen.[*]

[*] *The Monastic Diurnal or Day Hours of the Monastic Breviary According to the Holy Rule of St Benedict with Additional Rubrics and Devotions for its Recitation in Accordance with the Book of Common Prayer* (Oxford University Press, 1957), 610.

ARCHANGEL GABRIEL

The Archangel Gabriel is remembered on 24 March, and also with Michael on 29 September.

Send thy archangel, Gabriel, the mighty;
Herald of heaven, may he from us mortals
Spurn the old serpent, watching o'er the temples
Where thou art worshipped.

Rabanus Maurus, trans. Percy Dearmer
'Christ, the Fair Glory of the Holy Angels', NEH 190, v. 3

We remember Gabriel mainly for his visits to Zechariah when he foretold the birth of John to Elizabeth. Zechariah was burning incense in the temple:

> There appeared to him an angel of the Lord, standing at the right side of the altar of incense. When Zechariah saw him, he was terrified; and fear overwhelmed him. But the angel said

> to him, 'Do not be afraid, Zechariah, for your prayer has been heard. Your wife Elizabeth will bear you a son, and you will name him John. You will have joy and gladness, and many will rejoice at his birth, for he will be great in the sight of the Lord. He must never drink wine or strong drink; even before his birth he will be filled with the Holy Spirit. He will turn many of the people of Israel to the Lord their God. (Luke 1:11–16)

The angel goes on to describe how the child, John will grow up, before identifying himself:

> Zechariah said to the angel, 'How will I know that this is so? For I am an old man, and my wife is getting on in years.' The angel replied, 'I am Gabriel. I stand in the presence of God, and I have been sent to speak to you and to bring you this good news. (Luke 1:18–19)

What awesome news—yet it was true, however unlikely it sounded—and we know that Zechariah was made dumb until the son was born.

Then Gabriel came to Mary to tell her she was to be the mother of God's son, Jesus.

> In the sixth month the angel Gabriel was sent by God to a town in Galilee called Nazareth, to a virgin engaged to a man whose name was Joseph, of the house of David. The virgin's name was Mary. And he came to her and said, 'Greetings, favoured one! The Lord is with you.' But she was much perplexed by his words and pondered what sort of greeting this might be. The angel said to her, 'Do not be afraid, Mary, for you have found favour with God.' (Luke 1:26–30)

Joseph, too, was unwilling to believe such news, until the angel came to tell him it was true. These were normal responses for any human—yet the news brought by the angel was impossible to ignore: this was a time to listen, ponder, act. That is something we often neglect to do.

Gabriel is also mentioned by name in the Book of Daniel:

> When I, Daniel, had seen the vision, I tried to understand it. Then someone appeared standing before me, having the appearance

> of a man, and I heard a human voice by the Ulai, calling, 'Gabriel, help this man understand the vision.' So he came near where I stood; and when he came, I became frightened and fell prostrate. But he said to me, 'Understand, O mortal, that the vision is for the time of the end.' (Dan. 8:15–17)

Daniel has had a vision and is confessing his sins and praying to God in the evening when Gabriel appears with a message for him:

> … while I was speaking in prayer, the man Gabriel, whom I had seen before in a vision, came to me in swift flight at the time of the evening sacrifice. He came and said to me, 'Daniel, I have now come out to give you wisdom and understanding. (Dan. 9:21–2)

We recall Gabriel each time we pray the Angelus—as it was the Archangel Gabriel who brought tidings to Mary.

Prayer

> O God, who from among other angels
> chose Archangel Gabriel to announce
> the mystery of the Incarnation
> mercifully grant that we who celebrate
> this feast on earth may experience
> his protection.*

---
* *Monastic Diurnal*, 500.

ARCHANGEL RAPHAEL

The Archangel Raphael is remembered in some churches on 24 October.

Send thy archangel, Raphael, the restorer
Of the misguided ways of men who wander,
Who at thy bidding strengthens soul and body
With thine anointing.
> Rabanus Maurus, trans. Percy Dearmer
> 'Christ, the Fair Glory of the Holy Angels', NEH 190, v. 4

Raphael is named in the Deuterocanonical book of Tobit:

> I was sent to you to test you. And at the same time God sent me to heal you and Sarah your daughter-in-law. I am Raphael, one of the seven angels who stand ready and enter before the glory of the Lord. (Tobit 12:14–15)

Raphael is mentioned numerous times in the apocryphal book of Enoch, which places him among the most important angels, along with Michael and Gabriel (Enoch 40:9; 54:6). In the first of these passages Raphael is the healer; in the second, he with Michael, Gabriel and Phanuel lead the wicked away to punishment. These four angels are often considered to be the four 'living creatures' of Ezekiel 1:5:

> As I looked, a stormy wind came out of the north: a great cloud with brightness around it and fire flashing forth continually, and in the middle of the fire, something like gleaming amber. In the middle of it was something like four living creatures. This was their appearance: they were of human form. Each had four faces, and each of them had four wings. (Ezek. 1:4–6)

The commonest image of an angel nowadays looks much more like a human with two wings.

Ezekiel chapter 1 describes the four angels in great detail. The idea of four principal angels appears again in Revelation:

> Around the throne, and on each side of the throne, are four living creatures, full of eyes in front and behind: the first living creature like a lion, the second living creature like an ox, the third living creature with a face like a human face, and the fourth living creature like a flying eagle. And the four living creatures, each of them with six wings, are full of eyes all around and inside. Day and night without ceasing they sing,
> 'Holy, holy, holy,
> the Lord God the Almighty,
> who was and is and is to come.' (Rev. 4:6–8)

We do not often think of that great passage of the Sanctus coming from such a vivid description of angels. Raphael is particularly important in Jewish medieval writings, but is an integral part of the Christian angelology as well. He is remembered as the Healer, the Curer of Ills.

> Then the angel showed me the river of the water of life, bright as crystal, flowing from the throne of God and of the Lamb through the middle of the street of the city. On either side of the river is the tree of life with its twelve kinds of fruit, producing its fruit each month; and the leaves of the tree are for the healing of the nations. (Rev. 22:1–2)

In this we might see the tree of life bearing leaves for the healing of the nations so important for the world today.

Prayer

> O God, who gave blessed Raphael, the Archangel, to thy servant Tobias as a comrade on his journey, grant unto us thy servants that we may always be protected by his watchfulness and defended by his help.*

---

* *Monastic Diurnal*, 634.

ARCHANGEL URIEL

The Archangel Uriel does not have a commemorative day of his own.

Although he is not named in the canonical Christian biblical texts, Uriel occupies an important place in the major apocryphal texts, particularly in 2 Esdras and the book of Enoch, in which he is listed as one of the seven angels who preside over the world. He is credited with a number of important and critical acts from the earliest stories of the Bible: he is traditionally the angel who drove Adam and Eve from the Garden of Eden with a flaming sword; he warned Noah about the impending flood:

> Then said the Most High, the Holy and Great One spake, and sent Uriel to the son of Lamech, and said to him: 'Go to Noah and tell him in my name "Hide thyself!" and reveal to him the

> end that is approaching: that the whole earth will be destroyed, and a deluge is about to come upon the whole earth, and will destroy all that is on it.' (Enoch 10:1–3)*

Uriel also reveals the judgement of the fallen angels (Enoch 19 and 21); in Jewish tradition he is the angel sent to check the doors of homes throughout Egypt for lamb's blood during Passover; and in Christian tradition rescues John the Baptist from the slaughter of the Holy Innocents, carrying John and his mother to join Jesus and his family in Egypt.

Uriel is seen as a saving angel, and is also known as the angel of wisdom, enlightenment and Divine Guidance; his help is often sought in decision-making, learning, and resolving conflicts, and is symbolized in art by a book, scroll, or flame. In some Anglican and Eastern Orthodox churches he serves as the patron saint of the arts and sciences for his ability to inspire and awaken the intellect.

Prayer

O holy angel Uriel, whose name means 'God is my Light', we pray that you will guide our thoughts and actions with the light of Christ. We ask that you guard and protect us against all the attacks of Satan, who has tempted us since the Garden of Eden.

---

* This translation is from *The Apocrypha and Pseudepigrapha of the Old Testament*, ed. Robert Henry Charles (The Clarendon Press, 1913). The book of Enoch was removed from the Hebrew Bible because it is inconsistent with the teachings of the Torah.

HOLY GUARDIAN ANGELS

The Holy Guardian Angels are remembered on 2 October.

I am going to send an angel in front of you, to guard you on the way and to bring you to the place that I have prepared.
(Ex. 23:20)

> For he will command his angels concerning you
>   to guard you in all your ways.
> On their hands they will bear you up,
>   so that you will not dash your foot against a stone.
(Ps. 91:11–12)

The Holy Guardian Angels protect us wherever we are, or wherever we go, in all and every circumstance. A happy thought! Yes, but it is more than a thought, for it is truth. God does send his angels to watch over us, as he always has—some as his messengers, some with healing and others to guard and guide us.

Lord, give thy angels every day
Command to guide us on our way,
And bid them every evening keep
Their watch around us while we sleep.

John M. Neale (1818–1866)
'Around the Throne of God', NEH 191, v. 3

I remember my maternal grandmother talking to me when I was a small child, not yet at school, and telling me about Guardian Angels. She said that we each have our own angel to watch over us and guide us on our way. We do not see the angel, but this Guardian Angel is always there. I have always remembered this, but I think I must often give my Guardian Angel a pretty hard time!

> Take care that you do not despise one of these little ones; for, I tell you, in heaven their angels continually see the face of my Father in heaven. (Matt. 18:10)

> The angel of the Lord encamps
>   around those who fear him, and delivers them. (Ps. 34:7)

Many of us were taught as children that when we die we will become angels; this is not a recent idea, and indeed is found in the Acts of the Apostles:

> On recognizing Peter's voice, she [the maid Rhoda] was so overjoyed that, instead of opening the gate, she ran in and announced that Peter was standing at the gate. They said to her, 'You are out of your mind!' But she insisted that it was so. They said, 'It is his angel.' (Acts 12:14–15)

When I entered Community as a young sister, Postulants were given a Novice, known as their 'Angel', to help and guide them in the practical ways and customs of the Community. These were earthly Guardian Angels.

We know that our spiritual Guardian Angel is always there to give us a nudge. While we know that God loves us always, wherever we are, no matter what our response may be, even so we may need a nudge, but we must recognize and listen, take heed—really hear, and *act* in response. This, of course, needs faith, trust and prayer on our part.

I don't say this with the expectation that we might suddenly change, but with an understanding that the next step along the way at home, in family, at work, in the Church or in Community, may become clear, and that we can accept it with thanksgiving for our Guardian Angel who gave us the nudge.

Safeguarding is very much on our minds these days, and we hear much about the safeguarding policy for all organizations, including religious communities. I wonder how it would be regarded if an organization were to make a statement saying: 'As our Safeguarding Policy we put our trust and faith in the help and guidance of our Guardian Angels'?

Let us give thanks for the Guardian Angels constantly doing the work God gives them with praise and adoration.

> Are not all angels spirits in the divine service, sent to serve for the sake of those who are to inherit salvation?   (Heb. 1:14)

Prayer

> O Lord God of Hosts, by whose command the holy angels are sent forth to guide and defend us; grant that, protected by their unceasing vigilance, we may live and work to your praise and glory. Amen.

LUCIFER AND HIS ANGELS

Lucifer's name comes from the Latin translation of his Hebrew name in Isaiah, 'Sataniel', which means 'Morning star', 'Day star' or 'Son of Dawn':

> How you are fallen from heaven,
> O Day Star, son of Dawn!
> How you are cut down to the ground,
> you who laid the nations low!
> You said in your heart,
> 'I will ascend to heaven; …
> I will make myself like the Most High.'
> But you are brought down to Sheol,
> to the depths of the Pit.   (Is. 14:12–13, 14–15)

The King James Version of the Bible renders Isaiah verse 12, 'How art thou fallen from heaven, O Lucifer, son of the morning!' Satan fell prey to ambition and the seduction of power.

> Then he [the king = God] will say to those at his left hand, 'You that are accursed, depart from me into the eternal fire prepared for the devil and his angels …'   (Matt. 25:41)

We may have Guardian Angels to watch over us, but we need to remember that the devil also has his angels who are ever ready to suggest ways of deflecting us from the true path of life in God. In the second letter to the Corinthians we are warned:

> Even Satan disguises himself as an angel of light.   (2 Cor. 11:14)

One of the things that we learn from the description of the expulsion of the angels is that nothing—even being close to God—can protect us from the consequences of our wrong actions. A passage in 2 Peter is filled with righteous anger and warning against sin and temptation, but it also tells us that if we have an ounce of goodness in us, if we stand up to those who try to make us follow the wrong path, then we can be saved.

> For if God did not spare the angels when they sinned, but cast them into hell and committed them to chains of deepest darkness to be kept until the judgment; and if he did not spare the ancient world, even though he saved Noah, a herald of righteousness, with seven others, when he brought a flood on a world of the ungodly; … then the Lord knows how to rescue the godly from trial, and to keep the unrighteous under punishment until the day of judgment — especially those who indulge their flesh in depraved lust, and who despise authority.
>
> Bold and willful, they are not afraid to slander the glorious ones, whereas angels, though greater in might and power, do not bring against them a slanderous judgment from the Lord.
>
> (2 Pet. 2:4–5, 9–11)

Just as with the angels of God, Lucifer's angels may not be readily identifiable. Saint Teresa of Àvila in chapter XXXI of her *Life* alludes to this, saying,

> I have seldom seen him [the devil] in bodily shape, but I have often seen him without any form, as in the kind of vision I have described, in which no form is seen but the object is known to be there.*

We need to listen carefully and ask for discernment to hear only the angels of light, and to make the right decisions.

> O measureless might,
> Ineffable love,
> While angels delight
> To hymn thee above,
> Thy humbler creation,
> Though feeble their lays,
> With true adoration
> Shall sing to thy praise.
>
> Robert Grant (1779–1838)
> 'O Worship the King', NEH 433, v. 6

---

* *The Life of Teresa of Jesus*, trans. E. Allison Peers (Bantam, 1996), 208.

THE HEAVENLY HOST

While the appearances of angels in the Bible that we recall most are of single angels, or perhaps two, and we might think mainly of the archangels or our Guardian Angel, there are many places in the Bible where we are told that angels and archangels are part of a great host of holy beings. On that first Christmas night a great choir of angels appeared in the heavens as the shepherds heard the news of the birth of Jesus:

> And suddenly there was with the angel a multitude of the heavenly host, praising God and saying,
> > 'Glory to God in the highest heaven,
> > and on earth peace among those whom he favors!'
> > > (Luke 2:13–14)

This is familiar to us from the well-known Christmas carol:

> Thus spake the seraph; and forthwith
> Appeared a shining throng
> Of angels praising God, who thus
> Addressed their joyful song:
> 'All glory be to God on high,
> And on the earth be peace;
> Good-will henceforth from heaven to men
> Begin and never cease.'
> > Nahum Tate (1652–1715)
> > 'While Shepherds Watched', NEH 42, vv. 5–6

Saint John, in his vision of Revelation that gives us so many of our images of angels, relates:

> Then I looked, and I heard the voice of many angels surrounding the throne and the living creatures and the elders; they numbered myriads of myriads and thousands of thousands … (Rev. 5:11)

> And all the angels stood around the throne and around the elders and the four living creatures, and they fell on their faces before the throne and worshipped God … (Rev. 7:11)

Angels are mentioned and celebrated in so many hymns, particularly those from the nineteenth century when there was an upsurge of interest in supernatural creatures.

Around the throne of God a band
of glorious angels ever stand;
Bright things they see, sweet harps they hold,
And on their heads are crowns of gold.

John M. Neale
'Around the Throne of God', NEH 191, v. 1

If you have heard children singing this hymn, you may have heard their version of line three: 'Bright things they see, sweet *hearts* they hold.' Children have a way of telling us truths in this way; the angels carry our hearts close to God in praise. May our hearts be full of that joy and love as we praise and worship God.

Angels come to mind particularly at Christmas when we celebrate the Feast of the Nativity. We encounter them as we hear the Nativity story told in words, pictures and plays. Children rush home to say 'I am going to be an angel in the play!', as pleased as if they were to be Mary or Joseph at the manger with Jesus.

Christmas cards of the Holy Family in a traditional manger scene with animals often include cherubs in the background, representing the angels, but appearing childlike, as if mirroring the Saviour as a baby. They remind us to praise and adore God with childlike simplicity. Many hymns that we sing at Christmas describe the angels' proclamation of the Incarnation, so let us, day by day, lift our hearts in prayer and praise with the angels to the glory of God.

Hark! the herald angels sing
Glory to the new-born King.

Charles Wesley (1707–1788)
'Hark! the Herald Angels Sing', NEH 26, chorus

ANGELS IN THE SCRIPTURES

The Bible has nearly 300 references to angels: they appear in seventeen books of the Old Testament and eighteen books of the New Testament. Often angels are important messengers, as in the announcements to the Virgin Mary and to her cousin Elizabeth about their pregnancies. Angels continued to visit the Holy family after the birth of Jesus, to keep them safe:

> ... an angel of the Lord appeared to Joseph in a dream and said, 'Get up, take the child and his mother, and flee to Egypt, and remain there until I tell you; for Herod is about to search for the child, to destroy him.' Then Joseph got up, took the child and his mother by night, and went to Egypt, and remained there until the death of Herod. (Matt. 2:13–15)

Joseph's actions saved his family, and when it was time to return from Egypt, an angel visited again:

> When Herod died, an angel of the Lord suddenly appeared in a dream to Joseph in Egypt and said, 'Get up, take the child and his mother, and go to the land of Israel, for those who were seeking the child's life are dead.' (Matt. 2:19–20)

Joseph trusted the angel and did he was told to do. His trust was based on a long tradition in Scripture of angels bringing important messages and leading the faithful out of danger, particularly in the powerful record of the book of Exodus, chapter 14, when the Angel of the Lord protected the Israelites from the Passover scourge, then went before them to lead them out of Egypt and, finally, after their long journey, brought them to the Promised Land.

> I am going to send an angel in front of you, to guard you on the way and to bring you to the place that I have prepared. Be attentive to him and listen to his voice; do not rebel against him, for he will not pardon your transgression; for my name is in him. But if you listen attentively to his voice and do all that I say, then I will be an enemy to your enemies and a foe to your foes. When my angel goes in front of you, and brings you to the Amorites, the Hittites, the Perizzites, the Canaanites, the Hivites, and the Jebusites, and I blot them out, you shall not bow down to their gods, or worship them, or follow their practices, but you shall utterly demolish them and break their pillars in pieces.
>
> (Ex. 23:20–4)

This is part of a passage following the giving of the Ten Commandments to Moses. The verses explain and enlarge on the Commandments. Here we read that if we obey the angel's instructions then all will be well; but if we disobey, think we know better, or just ignore an angel, then misery and hardship will come to us.

In chapter 2 of Revelation, messages are sent to different angels to give to their respective churches, or congregations.

> To the angel of the church in Ephesus write: These are the words of him who holds the seven stars in his right hand, who walks among the seven golden lampstands: 'I know your works, your toil and your patient endurance.' (Rev. 2:1–2)

Messages are also sent to the 'angels' of the churches in Smyrna, Pergamum, Thyatira, Sardis, Philadelphia and Laodicea. The way the messages are worded suggests these angels were actually temporal spiritual leaders, perhaps like early bishops.

Trust

The story of the burning, fiery furnace tells of Nebuchadnezzar's astonishment when Daniel's companions Shadrach, Meshach and Abednego, who had been put into the furnace because they would not deny God, were joined by a fourth person, and were not burned.

> Then King Nebuchadnezzar was astonished and rose up quickly. He said to his counselors, 'Was it not three men that we threw bound into the fire?' They answered the king, 'True, O king.' He replied, 'But I see four men unbound, walking in the middle of the fire, and they are not hurt; and the fourth has the appearance of a god.' (Dan. 3:24–5)

The three men stepped out of that fiery furnace alive and well, saved by an angel whom God had sent to protect them, and King Nebuchadnezzar recognized the angel for what it was:

> Nebuchadnezzar said, 'Blessed be the God of Shadrach, Meshach, and Abednego, who has sent his angel and delivered his servants who trusted in him.' (Dan. 3:28)

This is an example of faith in God and of how angels are sent to protect us: the faith of Daniel's friends that all would be well if they trusted and obeyed God saved them. Such trust is a great lesson to us, especially when things seem difficult or impossible: simply trust and obey.

Trust is often the most difficult thing for humans, but there are extraordinary examples in the Scriptures. In Genesis chapter 22, we hear of Abraham's faith and obedience when God tested him by asking him to offer his son Isaac as a sacrifice. How many other people asked to sacrifice their child would even begin to make the necessary preparations, let alone set out on the journey to the place of sacrifice? Abraham trusted and obeyed; he trusted in his God:

> Then Abraham reached out his hand and took the knife to kill his son. But the angel of the Lord called to him from heaven, and said, 'Abraham, Abraham!' And he said, 'Here I am.' He said, 'Do not lay your hand on the boy or do anything to him; for now I know that you fear God, since you have not withheld your son, your only son, from me.' (Gen. 22:10–12)

We may not be tested in such a dramatic way, but in small simple, everyday things, as well as in bigger decisions: shall I take that job; shall I try my vocation as a priest or Religious; should I say 'yes' to that marriage proposal? These are not easy decisions and they call for prayerful discernment, trust and faith.

Whoever we are, or wherever we are, and whatever our problem, God loves us as we are and where we are and is ever wanting to help us. However, too often we do not respond in loving adoration, we do not listen to God's angels, but try to do things on our own, in our way. We ought not to be surprised, then, when things do not go our way: we have forgotten to stop, be still, listen and ponder—to meditate before deciding. We are slow to learn.

Do Not Be Afraid

In the Gospels of Matthew, Mark and Luke, we are told of Mary Magdalen and Mary the mother of James going to the sepulchre after the Sabbath. Although perplexed and upset to find the tomb empty, the women were more afraid of the angel who appeared to them. In Matthew and Mark the angel tells them, 'Do not be afraid!',

> the angel said to the women, 'Do not be afraid; I know that you are looking for Jesus who was crucified. He is not here; for he has been raised, as he said. Come, see the place where he lay. Then go quickly and tell his disciples, "He has been raised from the dead, and indeed he is going ahead of you to Galilee; there you will see him." This is my message for you.' So they left the tomb quickly with fear and great joy, and ran to tell his disciples.
>
> (Matt. 28:5–8)

Good News, but almost unbelievable news. Yet, it really was true, for Jesus met them on the way:

> Suddenly Jesus met them and said, 'Greetings!' And they came to him, took hold of his feet, and worshipped him. Then Jesus said to them, 'Do not be afraid; go and tell my brothers to go to Galilee; there they will see me.'
>
> (Matt. 28:9–10)

Twice they heard 'Do not be afraid'. So often it is fear that causes us to question, to doubt—it is fear that says 'It can't be true'. It tests our faith, our trust, our love. In these situations, we need to listen for the voice of the angel telling us, 'Do not be afraid!'

> And God heard the voice of the boy; and the angel of God called to Hagar from heaven, and said to her, 'What troubles you, Hagar? Do not be afraid…' (Gen. 21:17)

> 'I am Raphael, one of the seven angels who stand ready and enter before the glory of the Lord.' The two of them were shaken; they fell face down, for they were afraid. But he said to them, 'Do not be afraid…' (Tobit 12:15–17)

> Then there appeared to him an angel of the Lord, standing at the right side of the altar of incense. When Zechariah saw him, he was terrified; and fear overwhelmed him. But the angel said to him, 'Do not be afraid…' (Luke 1:11–13)

> In the sixth month the angel Gabriel was sent by God to a town in Galilee called Nazareth, to a virgin engaged to a man whose name was Joseph, of the house of David. The virgin's name was Mary. And he came to her and said, 'Greetings, favoured one! The Lord is with you.' But she was much perplexed by his words and pondered what sort of greeting this might be. The angel said to her, 'Do not be afraid…' (Luke 1:26–30)

> In that region there were shepherds living in the fields, keeping watch over their flock by night. Then an angel of the Lord stood before them, and the glory of the Lord shone around them, and they were terrified. But the angel said to them, 'Do not be afraid…' (Luke 2:8–10)

> For last night there stood by me an angel of the God to whom I belong and whom I worship, and he said, 'Do not be afraid…' (Acts 27:23–4)

ANGEL PRAYERS AND QUOTATIONS

Prayers

A Child's Bedtime Prayer

Now I lay me down to sleep
I pray the Lord my soul to keep.
Angels watch me through the night,
And keep me in thy blessed sight. Amen

There are many versions of this; the earliest is by
George Wheler (1651–1724) in *The Protestant Monastery* (1698)

Nursery Rhyme

Matthew, Mark, Luke and John,
Bless the bed that I lie on.
Four corners to my bed,
Four angels round my head.
One to watch and one to pray,
And two to bear my soul away.

Sabine Baring-Gould (1834–1924)

Before Beginning a Journey

May God send
Six angels to bless us,
Two in front, two behind,
And two to guard, and guide us on our way.

Traditional

Evening Prayer

When at night I go to sleep,
Fourteen angels watch do keep:
Two my head are guarding,
Two my feet are guiding,
Two are on my right hand,
Two are on my left hand,
Two who warmly cover,
Two who o'er me hover,
Two to whom 'tis given
to guide my steps to heaven.

Adelheid Wette (1858–1916)
'Evening Prayer' from the opera *Hansel and Gretel* (1892)

A Prayer used at Compline, also used at a House Blessing

Visit this place, O Lord, we pray,
And drive far from it the snares of the enemy;
May your holy angels dwell with us
And guard us in peace,
And may your blessing be always upon us;
Through Jesus Christ our Lord. Amen.

Common Worship

An Evening/Bedtime Prayer

In the name of God, may Michael,
the protection of God, be at my right hand,
and Gabriel, the power of God at my left,
before me Uriel the light of God,
behind me Raphael the healing of God:
and above me the presence of God. Amen.

Jewish bedtime prayer: the 'Angelic Invocation
for Divine Protection', from the *Kriyat Shema al HaMitah*

Quotations

Angels are the 'greenest' of all beings, since they leave no footprint, carbon or otherwise, they travel on their own wings. We cannot compete with that mode of travel, but we could travel on the wings of prayer, at any time of the day or night.

Modern Saying.

St Gregory the Great, seeing some British slaves on sale in the market in Rome, was impressed by their fair hair, a rare sight in Italy, and asked who they were. 'Angli,' he was told—people from Anglia. 'Non Angli, sed angeli,' he replied—'not Angles, but angels.'

Venerable Bede, Historia ecclesiastica gentis Anglorum (AD 731).

The angels are so enamoured of the language that is spoken in heaven, that they will not distort their lips with the hissing and unmusical dialects of men, but speak their own, whether there be any who understand it or not.

Ralph Waldo Emerson (1803–1882)
Essay on 'Intellect', in Essays, Lectures and Orations (William S. Orr and Co., 1848), 182.

The wings of angels are often found on the backs of the least likely people.

Eric Honeycutt
The Quote Garden 'Create your own Quote' Contest 2011.

The golden moments in the stream of life rush past us, and we see nothing but sand; the angels come to visit us, and we only know them when they are gone.

George Eliot (1819–1880)
from 'Janet's Repentance', in The Works of George Eliot: Scenes of Clerical Life, vol. II (William Blackwood & Sons, 1878), 109.

It was pride that changed angels into devils; it is humility that makes men as angels.
Attributed to Saint Augustine (354–430)
in *Manipulus Florum*, ed. Thomas Hibernicus (Piacenza, 1483).

Angels can fly because they can take themselves lightly.
Gilbert K. Chesterton (1874–1936)
Orthodoxy (John Lane Company, 1908/1911), 223.

No Place so Sacred from such Fops is Barr'd.
Nor is *Paul's Church* more safe than *Paul's Church-yard*:
Nay, run to *Altars; there* they'll talk you dead;
For *Fools* rush in where *Angels* fear to tread.
Alexander Pope (1688–1744)
An Essay on Criticism (Printed for W. Lewis, 1711), 36.

It is not because Angels are Holier than Men or Devils that makes them Angels, but because they do not Expect Holiness from one another, but from God only.
William Blake (1757–1827)
from [A Vision of The Last Judgment],
in *The Poetry and Prose of William Blake* (Doubleday, 1965), 565.

The teachers of morality: they discourse like angels, but they live like men.
Samuel Johnson (1709–1784)
The History of Rasselas, Prince of Abyssinia
(R. and J. Dodsley, 1759), chapter XVIII.

An ICM poll shows that one in three people questioned believe in guardian angels, and one in ten report seeing angels. In another survey, for the think-tank Theos, 21% of those who never worship in church confess they believe in angels, along with (in a different study) seven per cent of atheists.
Peter Stanford (1961–)
'One in Three of Us Now Believes in Guardian
Angels. What's Going On?' *The Article*, 4 March 2019.

Picture Credits

Many pictures reproduced in this book were sourced through Wikimedia Commons. The publishers have made every effort to ensure these images are rights-free, and apologize to any creator for inadvertent unauthorized use of their image. Details of licences cited below may be found here: https://creativecommons.org/share-your-work/cclicenses/

Page

Frontispiece: Charles Robinson, illustration in *Andersen's Fairy Tales* (Dent, 1899).

1   Hendrik Peeters (1815–1869), 'Angels Making Music', wooden sculptures, *c.* 1866, pulpit canopy, Sint-Antonius Kathedraal, Breda, Netherlands (image by ReneeWrites, CC-BY-4.0).

1–40 *passim:* Giuseppe Sammartino (1720–1793) and his pupils, crèche angel figures, terracotta, wood, wire and fabrics, second half of the 18th century, in collection 'Nativity Scenes of Naples', Metropolitan Museum of Art, New York, USA (public domain).

2   William Blake (1757–1827), 'Jacob's Dream', pen, ink and watercolour, 1805, British Museum, London, UK, object ID: P_1949-1112-2 (public domain).

4   James Tissot (1836–1902), 'Madeleine dans le tombeau interroge les anges' ('Mary Magdalene Questions the Angels in the Tomb'), watercolour, *c.* 1890, Brooklyn Museum, New York, artwork ID: 13521 (public domain).

5   Annibale Carracci (1560–1609), 'Holy Women at Christ's Tomb', oil on canvas, *c.* 1590s, Hermitage Museum, St Petersburg, Russia (public domain).

6   'Cherubim', mosaic, 12th century, Monreale Cathedral, Palermo, Sicily (CC-BY-2.5), edited image.

44

7   Iconographer Georgis, disciple of Theophanes the Cretan (1490–1559), painting, Monastery of Dionysius, Mount Athos, Greece (public domain).

8   Sandro Botticelli (1445–1510), 'Mystic Nativity', oil on canvas, 1500, National Gallery, London NG1034 (public domain).

9   Orthodox Icon, 'Christ Enthroned with Saints Mary the Mother of God, John the Baptist and Archangels Michael and Gabriel', from the icon of saints connected to Switzerland, tempera on wood, 21st century, Russian Orthodox Church of the Resurrection, Zürich, Switzerland (CC-BY-4.0).

11 Giuseppe Torretto (1661–1743), 'Archangels Gabriel, Michael, Raphael, Sealtiel', marble, interior of Chiesa dei Gesuiti (Santa Maria Assunta), Venice, Italy (photos: Didier Descouens, CC-BY-4.0).

12 James Powell and Sons of the Whitefriars Foundry, 'St Michael', mosaic, 1888, St John's Church, Boreham Road, Warminster, Wiltshire, UK (public domain).

14 Archangels 'Gabriel', 'Jeremiel', Raphael', 'Michael', 'Uriel', relief carvings on the font, 15th century, St Martinskirche, Seelze, Germany (photos: Georgius01, CC-BY-SA-3.0).

15 James Powell and Sons of the Whitefriars Foundry, 'St Gabriel', mosaic, 1888, St John's Church, Boreham Road, Warminster (public domain).

17 Leonardo da Vinci (1452–1519), 'Annunciation', oil on panel, c. 1472, Uffizi Gallery, Florence, Federico Zeri Foundation image ID 34358 (CC-BY-SA-4.0).

18 James Powell and Sons of the Whitefriars Foundry, 'St Raphael', mosaic, 1888, St John's Church, Boreham Road, Warminster (public domain).

19 Edward Burne-Jones (1833–1898), 'An Angel Playing a Flageolet', oil and tempera on paper, 1878, Sudley House, Aigburth, Liverpool, UK (public domain).

21 James Powell and Sons of the Whitefriars Foundry, 'St Uriel', mosaic, 1888, St John's Church, Boreham Road, Warminster (public domain).

22 Hardman & Co., 'Archangel Uriel Holding a Book', detail of stained-glass window, 1892, Beverley Minster, Yorkshire, UK (photo: Jules Guffogg and Jenny Hannan, CC-BY-2.0).

23 Андрей Николаевич Миронов (Andrey N. Mironov), 'Guardian Angel', oil on canvas, 2025, collection of the artist, Ryazan, Russia (CC0-1.0).

25 Melozzo da Forlì (1438–1494), 'Musician Angels', fresco, c. 1480, from the Basilica dei Santi Apostoli, now in Pinacoteca Vaticana, Vatican City (CC-BY-SA-4.0).

26 Limbourg brothers (fl. 1402–1416), 'The Fall of the Rebel Angels', tempera on vellum, Musée Condé, Chantilly, France, MS. 65, f. 64^v (public domain).

28 Guillaume Geefs (1805–1883), 'Le génie du mal [Lucifer]' marble, 1848, pulpit of St Paul's Cathedral, Liège, Belgium (photo: Luc Viatour / https://Lucnix.be CC-BY-SA-3.0)

31 Morris & Co. & Burne-Jones, 'St Michael Window', stained glass executed by Clayton & Bell, 1875, North Transept, Christ Church Cathedral, Oxford, UK (CC-BY-SA 3.0).

32 'Angel with St Joseph', stained glass, Church of the Annunciation, Nazareth, Israel (photo: Dennis Jarvis, 2016, free use, CC-BY-SA 2.0).

34 'The Fiery Furnance', mosaic, 11th century, Byzantine Monastery of Hosios Loukas, Greece (public domain).

35 Louis Desplaces (1682–1739), 'The Sacrifice of Isaac or Ismael', etching and engraving, undated, Metropolitan Museum of Art, New York, object number: 30.22(7.1) (public domain).

36 Joos van Cleve (c. 1485–1540/1), 'Angel of the Annunciation', from Triptych with the Lamentation of Christ, oil on panel, 1524, Städel Museum, Frankfurt am Main, Germany, accession number 803BR (public domain).

Bruges (?) Master c. 1485–90, 'Angel of the Annunciation', oil on oak panel, c. 1485–1490, Städel Museum, Frankfurt am Main, accession number 802D (public domain).

Achille Pertelli (1822–1891), 'Archangel Michael and the Dragon', painted glass, 1904, Holy Cross Chapel, Salt Lake City, Utah, USA (photo: Nate Bergin CC-BY-4.0).

Attributed to Jean de Liège (c. 1330–1381), 'Angel of the Annunciation', stone sculpture, c. 1370–90, Metropolitan Museum of Art, New York, object number: 17.190.390 (public domain).

37 Stephen Dykes Bower (1903–1994), 'Angel', wood carving on oak stalls, 1962, St Edmundsbury Cathedral, Bury St Edmunds, UK (public domain).

Edwin Blashfield (1848–1936), 'Angel with the Flaming Sword', oil on canvas, 1890–91, The Episcopal Church of the Ascension, Manhattan, New York, USA (public domain).

'Saint Uriel, Interpreter of Prophecies', painted panel, c. 1940, St Michael and All Angels Church, Howick, Northumberland, UK (photo: Loz Pycock CC-BY-SA-2.0).

Workshop of Lucas Cranach the Elder (1472–1553), 'Archangel Michael', oil on panel, c. 1535–45, private collection (public domain).

Glass factory of Emperor William II of Prussia, 'Angel & Shepherds', stained glass, 1893, Evangelical Lutheran Christmas Church, Bethlehem, Palestine (photo: James Emery, public domain).

38 William Morris & Co., 'Peace Angel', stained glass, c. 1900, St Gregory's Church, Vale of Lune, Cumbria, UK (public domain, CC-BY-2.0).

43 Hans Memling (1430–1494), 'The Annunciation', oil on panel, transferred to canvas, c. 1480–89, Metropolitan Museum of Art, New York, object number: 1975.1.113 (public domain).

44 Christmas 2020 lights in Regent Street, London (photo: Alex Live, CC0-1.0 Universal).

SLG PRESS PUBLICATIONS

FP1	*Prayer and the Life of Reconciliation*	Gilbert Shaw (1969)
FP2	*Aloneness not Loneliness*	Mother Mary Clare SLG (1969)
FP4	*Intercession*	Mother Mary Clare SLG (1969)
FP8	*Prayer: Extracts from the Teaching of Father Gilbert Shaw*	Gilbert Shaw (1973)
FP12	*Learning to Pray*	Mother Mary Clare SLG (1970, rev. 3/2025)
FP15	*Death, the Gateway to Life*	Gilbert Shaw (1971, 3/2024)
FP16	*The Victory of the Cross*	Dumitru Stăniloae (1970, 3/2023)
FP26	*The Message of Saint Seraphim*	Irina Gorainov (1974)
FP28	*Julian of Norwich: Four Studies to Commemorate the Sixth Centenary of the Revelations of Divine Love* Sister Benedicta Ward SLG, Sister Eileen Mary SLG, Sister Mary Paul SLG, A. M. Allchin (1973, 3/2022)	
FP43	*The Power of the Name: The Jesus Prayer in Orthodox Spirituality*	Kallistos Ware (1974)
FP46	*Prayer and Contemplation* and *Distractions are for Healing*	Robert Llewelyn (1975, rev. 4/2025)
FP48	*The Wisdom of the Desert Fathers*	trans. Sister Benedicta Ward SLG (1975)
FP50	*Letters of Saint Antony the Great*	trans. Derwas Chitty (1975, 2/2021)
FP54	*From Loneliness to Solitude*	Roland Walls (1976)
FP55	*Theology and Spirituality*	Andrew Louth (1976, rev. 1978, 3/2024)
FP61	*Kabir: The Way of Love and Paradox*	Sister Rosemary SLG (1977)
FP62	*Anselm of Canterbury: A Monastic Scholar*	Sister Benedicta Ward SLG (1973, 2/2024)
FP67	*Mary and the Mystery of the Incarnation: An Essay on the Mother of God in the Theology of Karl Barth*	Andrew Louth (1977, 2/2024)
FP68	*Trinity and Incarnation in Anglican Tradition*	A. M. Allchin (1977, rev. 2/2025)
FP70	*Facing Depression*	Gonville ffrench-Beytagh (1978, 2/2020)
FP71	*The Single Person*	Philip Welsh (1979)
FP72	*The Letters of Ammonas, Successor of St Antony*	trans. Derwas Chitty, introd. Sebastian Brock (1979, 2/2023)
FP74	*George Herbert, Priest and Poet*	Kenneth Mason (1980)
FP75	*A Study of Wisdom: Three Tracts by the Author of The Cloud of Unknowing*	trans. Clifton Wolters (1980)
FP81	*The Psalms: Prayer Book of the Bible*	Dietrich Bonhoeffer, trans. Sister Isabel SLG (1982, rev. 3/2025)
FP82	*Prayer & Holiness: The Icon of Man Renewed in God*	Dumitru Stăniloae (1982, rev. 2/2023)
FP85	*Walter Hilton: Eight Chapters on Perfection & Angels' Song*	trans. Rosemary Dorward (1983, rev. 3/2024)
FP88	*Creative Suffering*	Iulia de Beausobre (1989)
FP90	*Bringing Forth Christ: Five Feasts of the Child Jesus by St Bonaventure*	trans. Eric Doyle OFM (1984, 3/2024)
FP92	*Gentleness in John of the Cross*	Thomas Kane (1985, rev. 2/2025)
FP94	*Saint Gregory Nazianzen: Selected Poems*	trans. John McGuckin (1986, 2/2024)
FP95	*The World of the Desert Fathers: Stories and Sayings from the Anonymous Series of the Apophthegmata Patrum*	trans. Columba Stewart OSB (1986, 2/2020)
FP104	*Growing Old with God*	Timothy N. Rudd (1988, 2/2020)
FP106	*Julian Reconsidered*	Kenneth Leech, Sister Benedicta Ward SLG (1988/ rev. 2/2024)
FP108	*The Unicorn: Meditations on the Love of God*	Harry Galbraith Miller (1989)

FP109	*The Creativity of Diminishment*	Sister Anke (1990)
FP110	*Called to be Priests*	Hugh Wybrew (1989, updated 2/2024)
FP111	*A Kind of Watershed: An Anglican Lay View of Sacramental Confession*	Christine North (1990, updated 2/2022)
FP116	*Jesus, the Living Lord*	Bishop Michael Ramsey (1992)
FP120	*The Monastic Letters of Saint Athanasius the Great*	trans. and introd. Leslie Barnard (1994, 2/2023)
FP122	*The Hidden Joy*	Sister Jane SLG, ed. Dorothy Sutherland (1994)
FP124	*Prayer of the Heart: An Approach to Silent Prayer and Prayer in the Night*	Alexander Ryrie (1995, 3/2020)
FP126	*Evelyn Underhill, Anglican Mystic: Two Centenary Essays*	A. M. Allchin, Bishop Michael Ramsey (1977, rev. 4/2025)
FP127	*Apostolate and the Mirrors of Paradox*	Sydney Evans, ed. Andrew Linzey & Brian Horne (1996)
FP128	*The Wisdom of Saint Isaac the Syrian*	Sebastian Brock (1997)
FP129	*Saint Thérèse of Lisieux: Her Relevance for Today*	Sister Eileen Mary SLG (1997)
FP130	*Expectations: Five Addresses for Those Beginning Ministry*	Sister Edmée SLG (1997, 2/2024)
FP131	*Scenes from Animal Life: Fables for the Enneagram Types*	Waltraud Kirschke, trans. Sister Isabel SLG (1998)
FP132	*Praying the Word of God: The Use of Lectio Divina*	Charles Dumont OCSO (1999)
FP133	*Love Unknown: Meditations on the Death and Resurrection of Jesus*	John Barton (1999, 2/2024)
FP134	*The Hidden Way of Love: Jean-Pierre de Caussade's Spirituality of Abandonment*	Barry Conaway (1999, rev. 2/2025)
FP135	*Shepherd and Servant: The Spiritual Theology of Saint Dunstan*	Douglas Dales (2000)
FP137	*Pilgrimage of the Heart*	Sister Benedicta Ward SLG (2001)
FP138	*Mixed Life*	Walter Hilton, trans. Rosemary Dorward (2001, enlarged rev. 3/2024)
FP139	*In the Footsteps of the Lord: The Teaching of Abba Isaiah of Scetis*	John Chryssavgis, Luke Penkett (2001, 2/2023)
FP140	*A Great Joy: Reflections on the Meaning of Christmas*	Kenneth Mason (2001)
FP141	*Bede and the Psalter*	Sister Benedicta Ward SLG (2002, 2/2024)
FP142	*Abhishiktananda: A Memoir of Dom Henri Le Saux*	Murray Rogers, David Barton (2003)
FP143	*Friendship in God: The Encounter of Evelyn Underhill & Sorella Maria of Campello*	A. M. Allchin (2003, rev. 2/2025)
FP144	*Christian Imagination in Poetry and Polity: Some Anglican Voices from Temple to Herbert*	Bishop Rowan Williams (2004)
FP145	*The Reflections of Abba Zosimas: Monk of the Palestinian Desert*	trans. and introd. John Chryssavgis (2005, 3/2022)
FP146	*The Gift of Theology: The Trinitarian Vision of Ann Griffiths and Elizabeth of Dijon*	A. M. Allchin (2005)
FP147	*Sacrifice and Spirit*	Bishop Michael Ramsey (2005)
FP148	*Saint John Cassian on Prayer*	trans. A. M. Casiday (2006, 2/2024)
FP149	*Hymns of Saint Ephrem the Syrian*	trans. Mary Hansbury (2006, 2/2024)
FP150	*Suffering: Why All this Suffering? What Do I Do about It?*	Reinhard Körner OCD, trans. Sister Avis Mary SLG (2006)
FP151	*A True Easter: The Synod of Whitby 664 AD*	Sister Benedicta Ward SLG (2007, 2/2023)
FP152	*Prayer as Self-Offering*	Alexander Ryrie (2007)
FP153	*From Perfection to the Elixir: How George Herbert Fashioned a Famous Poem*	Benedick de la Mare (2008, 2/2024)
FP154	*The Jesus Prayer: Gospel Soundings*	Sister Pauline Margaret CHN (2008)

FP 155	*Loving God Whatever: Through the Year with Sister Jane*	Sister Jane SLG (2006)
FP 156	*Prayer and Meditation for a Sleepless Night*	
		SISTERS OF THE LOVE OF GOD (1993, 3/2024)
FP 157	*Being There: Caring for the Bereaved*	John Porter (2009)
FP 158	*Learn to Be at Peace: The Practice of Stillness*	Andrew Norman (2010)
FP 159	*From Holy Week to Easter*	George Pattison (2010)
FP 160	*Strength in Weakness: The Scandal of the Cross*	John W. Rogerson (2010)
FP 161	*Augustine Baker: Frontiers of the Spirit*	Victor de Waal (2010, rev. 2/2025)
FP 162	*Out of the Depths*	
		Gonville ffrench-Beytagh; epilogue Wendy Robinson (1990, 2/2010)
FP 163	*God and Darkness: A Carmelite Perspective*	
		Gemma Hinricher OCD, trans. Sister Avis Mary SLG (2010)
FP 164	*The Gift of Joy*	Curtis Almquist SSJE (2011)
FP 165	*'I Have Called You Friends': Suggestions for the Spiritual Life Based on the Farewell Discourses of Jesus*	Reinhard Körner OCD (2012)
FP 166	*Leisure*	Mother Mary Clare SLG (2012)
FP 167	*Carmelite Ascent: An Introduction to Saint Teresa and Saint John of the Cross*	
		Mother Mary Clare SLG (1973, rev. 2/2012)
FP 168	*Ann Griffiths and Her Writings*	Llewellyn Cumings (2012)
FP 169	*The Our Father*	Sister Benedicta Ward SLG (2012)
FP 171	*The Spiritual Wisdom of the Syriac Book of Steps*	Robert A. Kitchen (2013)
FP 172	*The Prayer of Silence*	Alexander Ryrie (2012)
FP 173	*On Tour in Byzantium: Excerpts from The Spiritual Meadow of John Moschus*	
		Ralph Martin SSM (2013)
FP 174	*Monastic Life*	Bonnie Thurston (2016)
FP 175	*Shall All Be Well? Reflections for Holy Week*	Graham Ward (2015)
FP 176	*Solitude and Communion: Papers on the Hermit Life*	ed. A. M. Allchin (2015)
FP 177	*The Prayers of Jacob of Serugh*	ed. Mary Hansbury (2015)
FP 178	*The Monastic Hours of Prayer*	Sister Benedicta Ward SLG (2016)
FP 179	*The Desert of the Heart: Daily Readings with the Desert Fathers*	
		trans. Sister Benedicta Ward SLG (2016)
FP 180	*In Company with Christ: Lent, Palm Sunday, Good Friday & Easter to Pentecost*	
		Sister Benedicta Ward SLG (2016)
FP 181	*Lazarus: Come Out! Reflections on John 11*	Bonnie Thurston (2017)
FP 182	*Unknowing & Astonishment: Meditations on Faith for the Long Haul*	
		Christopher Scott (2018)
FP 183	*Pondering, Praying, Preaching: Romans 8*	Bonnie Thurston (2019, 2/2021)
FP 184	*Shem'on the Graceful: Discourse on the Solitary Life*	
		trans. and introd. Mary Hansbury (2020)
FP 185	*God Under My Roof: Celtic Songs and Blessings*	Esther de Waal (2020)
FP 186	*Journeying with the Jesus Prayer*	James F. Wellington (2020)
FP 187	*Poet of the Word: Re-reading Scripture with Ephraem the Syrian*	Aelred Partridge OC (2020)
FP 188	*Identity and Ritual*	Alan Griffiths (2021)
FP 189	*River of the Spirit: The Spirituality of Simon Barrington-Ward*	Andy Lord (2021)
FP 190	*Prayer and the Struggle against Evil*	John Barton, Daniel Lloyd,
		James Ramsay, Alexander Ryrie (2021)
FP 191	*Dante's Spiritual Journey: A Reading of the Divine Comedy*	Tony Dickinson (2021)
FP 192	*Jesus the Undistorted Image of God*	John Townroe (2022)
FP 193	*Our Deepest Desire: Prayer, Fasting & Almsgiving in the Writings of Saint Augustine of Hippo*	Sister Susan SLG (2022)

FP194	*Lent with George Herbert*	Tony Dickinson (2022)
FP195	*Four Ways to the Cross*	Tony Dickinson (2022)
FP196	*Anselm of Canterbury, Teacher of Prayer*	Sister Benedicta Ward SLG (2022)
FP197	*With One Heart and Mind: Prayers out of Stillness*	Anthony Kemp (2023)
FP198	*Sayings of the Urban Fathers & Mothers*	James Ashdown (2023)
FP199	*Doors*	Sister Raphael SLG (2023)
FP200	*Monastic Vocation* SISTERS OF THE LOVE OF GOD,	Bishop Rowan Williams (2021)
FP201	*An Ecology of the Heart: Faith Through the Climate Crisis*	Duncan Forbes (2023)
FP202	*'In the image of the Image': Gregory of Nyssa's Opposition to Slavery*	Adam Couchman (2023)
FP203	*Gregory of Nyssa and the Sins of Asia Minor*	Jonathan Farrugia (2023)
FP204	*Discovery*	Arthur Bell (2023)
FP205	*Living Healing: the Spirituality of Leanne Payne*	Andy Lord (2023)
FP206	*Still Listening: Sowing the Seeds of the Jesus Prayer*	Bruce Batstone CJN (2023)
FP207	*Julian of Norwich: Four Essays to Commemorate 650 Years of the Revelations of Divine Love*	Bishop Graham Usher, Father Colin CSWG, Sister Elizabeth Ruth Obbard OC, Mother Hilary Crupi OJN (2023)
FP208	*TIME*	Dumitru Stăniloae, Kallistos Ware (2023)
FP209	*Pearls of Life: A Lifebelt for the Spirit*	Tony Dickinson (2024)
FP210	*The Way and the Truth and the Life: An Exploration by a Follower of the Way*	James Ramsay (2024)
FP211	*Cosmos, Crisis & Christ: Essays of Wendy Robinson*	Wendy Robinson (2024)
FP212	*Towards a Theology of Psychotherapy: The Spirituality of Wendy Robinson*	Andrew Louth (2024)
FP213	*Immersed in God and the World: Living Priestly Ministry*	Andy Lord (2024)
FP214	*The Road to Emmaus: A Sculptor's Journey through Time*	Rodney Munday (2024)
FP215	*Prayer Too Deep for Words*	Sister Edmée SLG (2024)
FP216	*The Prayers of St Isaac of Nineveh*	Sebastian Brock (2024)
FP217	*Two Medieval English Saints: Cuthbert and Alban*	Sister Benedicta Ward SLG (2024)
FP218	*Encountering the Depths*	Mother Mary Clare SLG (1981, rev. 3/2024)
FP219	*Conflict and Concord*	Sister Susan SLG, Bishop Humphrey Southern, Bronwen Neil, Sister Rosemary SLG, Sister Clare-Louise SLG (2024)
FP220	*Divine Love in the Song of Songs*	Sister Edmée SLG (2024)
FP221	*Zeal for the Faith: An Introduction to Christian-Muslim Dialogue*	Tony Dickinson (2024)
FP222	*Bernard & Abelard*	Sister Edmée SLG (2024)
FP223	*Eliot's Transitions: T. S. Eliot's Search for Identity and the Society of the Sacred Mission at Kelham Hall*	Vincent Strudwick (2024)
FP224	*Landscape, Soul and Spirit: Ecology, Prayer and Robert Macfarlane*	Andy Lord (2025)
FP225	*Our Home is in God*	John Townroe (2025)
FP226	*Signs of the Times: A Brief Survey of the Bible's Apocalyptic Writings*	Tony Dickinson (2025)
FP227	*And We Shall be Changed: Christian Reflections on Death and Dying*	James Ramsay (2025)
FP228	*Journeys into the Bible*	Sister Edmée SLG (2025)
FP229	*Directions*	Sister Edmée SLG (2025)

www.slgpress.co.uk

Contemplative Poetry Series

CP1	*Amado Nervo: Poems of Faith and Doubt*	trans. John Gallas (2021)
CP2	*Anglo-Saxon Poets: The High Roof of Heaven*	trans. John Gallas (2021)
CP3	*Middle English Poets: Where Grace Grows Ever Green*	ed. John Gallas (2021)
CP4	*The Voice inside Our Home: Selected Poems*	Edward Clarke (2022)
CP5	*Women & God: Drops in the Sea of Time*	trans. and ed. John Gallas (2022)
CP6	*Gabrielle de Coignard & Vittoria Colonna: Fly Not Too High*	trans. John Gallas (2022)
CP7	*Chancing on Sanctity: Selected Poems*	James Ramsay (2022)
CP8	*Gabriela Mistral: This Far Place*	trans. John Gallas (2023)
CP9	*Henry Vaughan & George Herbert: Divine Themes and Celestial Praise*	ed. Edward Clarke (2023)
CP10	*Love Will Come with Fire: Anthology*	Sisters of the Love of God (2023)
CP11	*Touchpapers: Anthology*	coll. and trans. John Gallas (2023)
CP12	*Seasons of my Soul: Selected Poems*	Clare McKerron (2023)
CP13	*Reinhard Sorge: Take Flight to God*	trans. John Gallas (2024)
CP14	*Embertide: Encountering Saint Frideswide*	Romola Parish (2024)
CP15	*Thomas Campion: Made All of Light*	ed. and introd. Julia Craig-McFeely (2024)
CP16	*When God Hides: Selected Poems*	Joseph Evans (2025)

Vestry Guides

VG1	*The Visiting Minister: How to Welcome Visiting Clergy to Your Church*	Paul Monk (2021)
VG2	*Help! No Minister! or Please Take the Service*	Paul Monk (2022)
VG3	*The Liturgy of the Eucharist: An Introductory Guide*	Paul Monk (2024)

www.slgpress.co.uk

The Sisters of the Love of God is an Anglican community of women religious living a contemplative monastic life.

To learn more about the Community and the Convent of the Incarnation at Fairacres, Oxford, see our website www.slg.org.uk.

As well as supporting those seeking to follow a vocation to the monastic life, the Community has a number of forms of association for those who feel drawn to share in the Sisters' life of prayer: Fellowship of the Love of God, Companions, Priests Associate or Oblate Sisters.

For more information email sisters@slg.org.uk or write to The Reverend Mother, Convent of the Incarnation, Parker Street, Oxford, OX4 1TB, UK.